The Bahá'í Faith

An Australian Aboriginal Perspective

Philip Obah (Guburu)

The Bahá'í Faith

An Australian Aboriginal Perspective

This book is dedicated

To my mother and family, my Ancestors the Wadja people, my wife, her family and her Ancestors, the Walmajarri people and also the Ngarti people for their spiritual guidance and insight.

To maintaining the knowledge and understanding of our Ancient Social and Spiritual Lores, which have been renewed through the vibrating influence of Bahá'u'lláh's New World Order.

To families that have passed onto the Abhá Kingdom and to all Aboriginal people in their struggle to keep unity amongst our people.

May they be guided to find the straight path.

The Aim

The aim of this book is to bring to the attention of Aboriginal and Torres Strait Islander people that a new message from God has appeared which has the remedy to fix not only the social and spiritual problems that we are facing but also the world.

It emphasises a renewed Spiritual Lore, maintaining our cultural identity, wisdom, knowledge and understanding from our ancestors in this ever embracing world.

This book is an invitation to all Aboriginal people to study this new divinely ordained Social and Spiritual Law for today, which "The Báb" and "Bahá'u'lláh" have released to humanity.

The Guardian of the Bahá'í Faith, Shoghi Effendi in his book Unfolding Destiny (page 365), spoke about how Indigenous people all over the world have a gift to share with the wider community, if they wish to sit, listen, learn and understand.

Shoghi Effendi wrote:

"A spiritual receptivity, a purity of heart and uprightness of character exists potentially amongst many of the peoples of the Pacific Isles to an extent equal to that of the tribesman of Africa. It is indeed an encouraging and awe-inspiring sight to witness the spread of our beloved Faith amongst those whom civilised nations misguidedly term "savages," "primitive people" and "uncivilised nations".

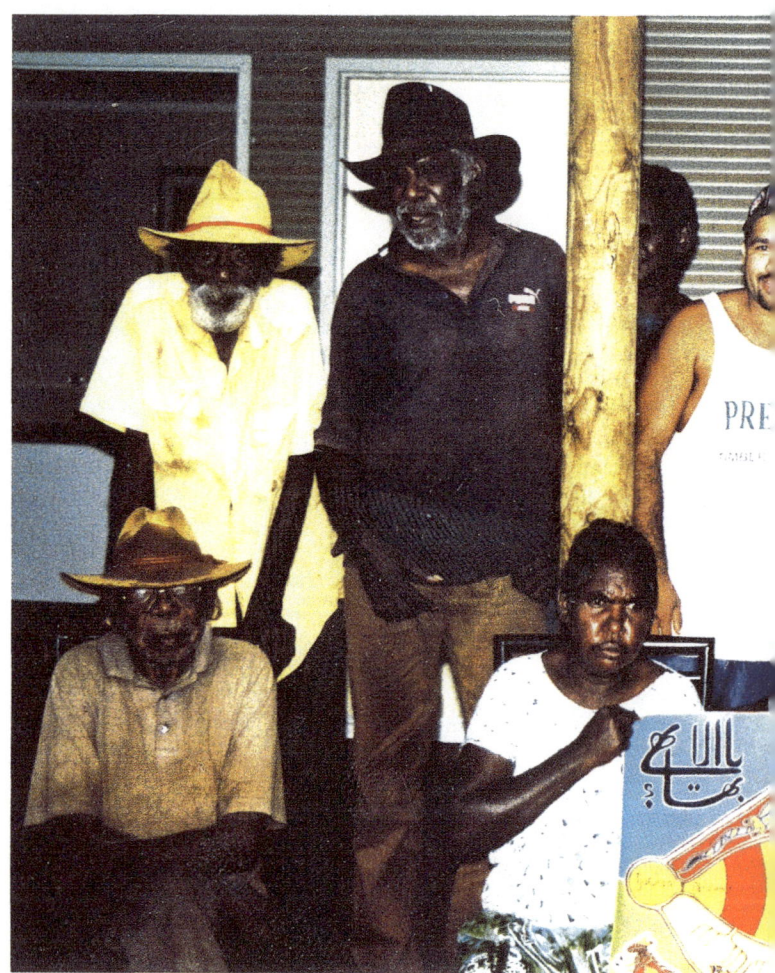

Role of Indigenous People

In the current Australian society and the rest of the world, the western culture has maintained its dominance over Aboriginal people.

It has been a long-standing assumption by western societies that indigenous peoples have nothing to offer or contribute to the development of the world wide community.

The Bahá'í Faith offers Aboriginal and Torres Strait Islander people a unique position at the forefront in teaching society a different perspective.

One of sharing our social lifestyle, spiritual knowledge, insight and understanding to improve the quality of life for all people including the downtrodden to fulfil their spiritual destiny.

"For the bedrock of the Bahá'í administrative order is the principle of unity in diversity, which has been so strongly and so repeatedly emphasized in the writings of the Cause."

(Shoghi Effendi: Dawn of a New Day, Page: 48)

These wonderful qualities and attributes that indigenous people have calls for the willingness of people to change within themselves, in both the Aboriginal and wider Australian community.

To rekindle the principles of our Social and Spiritual Lores, extended family kinship system, respect for Elders, caring, sharing, and insight.

A letter dated 25th July 1998, written on behalf of the Universal House of Justice to a National Spiritual Assembly states:

"The Universal House of Justice supports the view that in every country the cultural traditions of the people should be observed within the Bahá'í community, as long as they are not contrary to the Teachings ...

Of course many cultural elements everywhere will inevitably disappear or be merged with related ones from their societies, yet the totality will achieve that promised diversity within world unity. We can expect much cultural diversity in the long period before the emergence of a world commonwealth of nations in the Golden Age of Bahá'u'lláh's new world order.

Much wisdom and tolerance will be required and much time must elapse until the advent of that great day."

To understand the connection between Aboriginal Lore and the Bahá'í Faith is to see it in its pure form, its spiritual simplicity, rather than any ordinary institution.

Like Aboriginal Lore, the Bahá'í Faith is not complicated, it is simple to understand, it is only man's inability to simplify things that makes it complicated.

Aboriginal people come from an oral culture, where the stories are passed on and accompanied through the visual arts, which tell both the physical and spiritual connection of an individual, family and community to the land.

The Progressive Revelation

Ancient Cycle - Tjukurpa
Baiame
Bunjil
Dhurramulan
Wandjina
Rainbow Serpent
Kangaroo/Emu

Adamic Cycle
Abraham
Krishna
Moses
Zoroaster
Buddha
Jesus
Muhammad

Bahá'í Cycle
The Báb
Bahá'u'lláh

The painting tells a story of the Progressive Revelation and how all the world religions connect to each other and the Ancient Cycle - Tjukurpa (Aboriginal Lore).

Our Ancestors and Elders held the Ancient Faith of God in their hearts to the present day.

The later religions broke the lore of God.

Today Bahá'u'lláh has revealed the new revelation which unifies all the religions and people of the world.

"Twin luminaries that heralded the advent of the Faith of the Báb, prophesied that at the appearance of the Promised One all things would be reversed, the last would be first, the first last."

Bahá'u'lláh: Kitáb-i-Aqdas: Notes, Pages: 239-240

This is the straight Path, the fixed and immovable foundation.

Bahá'u'lláh: Gleanings, Page: 215

"Think not that We have revealed unto you a mere code of laws. Nay, rather, We have unsealed the choice Wine with the fingers of might and power. To this beareth witness that which the Pen of Revelation hath revealed. Meditate upon this, O men of insight!"

Bahá'u'lláh: The Kitáb-i-Aqdas, Page: 21

The Bahá'í Faith ~ An Australian Aboriginal Perspective

Recognition of "The Souls of God" in the Ancient Cycle

The Aboriginal and Torres Strait Islander people have been waiting for the day when both the eastern and western societies would recognise "The Souls of God" who walked this land, giving Aboriginal and Torres Strait Islander people the lore/law of God.

The Universal House of Justice termed them the "Souls of God" as the message they taught in the land did not travel to another land where thousands of people from all parts of the world joined or followed the social and spiritual lore/law of the Aboriginal and Torres Strait Islander people.

However, the recognition that Aboriginal and Torres Strait Islander people did receive the Lore/Law of God, came from Bahá'u'lláh Himself and now the National Spiritual Assembly of the Bahá'ís of Australia and the Continental Board of Counsellors of Australasia.

This recognition came in the form of a letter from the National Spiritual Assembly of the Bahá'ís of Australia to the National Spiritual Assembly of the Bahá'ís of Hawaii.

An extract of this letter dated 21 December 2001, addressing the "Fire in the Pacific" conference, where the National Spiritual Assembly stated:

"We take this opportunity to honor with humble admiration to indigenous friends throughout the Pacific whose spiritual example is a constant source of strength and inspiration to us. Our own indigenous representatives bring with them the stirrings of this land in recognition that the Royal Falcon has risen to fulfil the promises of the Ancient Cycle in bringing a new lore that binds and unites the hearts of all peoples and nations."

This is that "Brand New Day" that Aboriginal and Torres Strait Islander people have been waiting for that the Blessed Beauty has brought us the true "Coming of the Light".

The Bahá'í Faith ~ An Australian Aboriginal Perspective

Tjukurpa - The Ancient Cycle

During the Ancient Cycle God appeared to Aboriginal people in many forms.

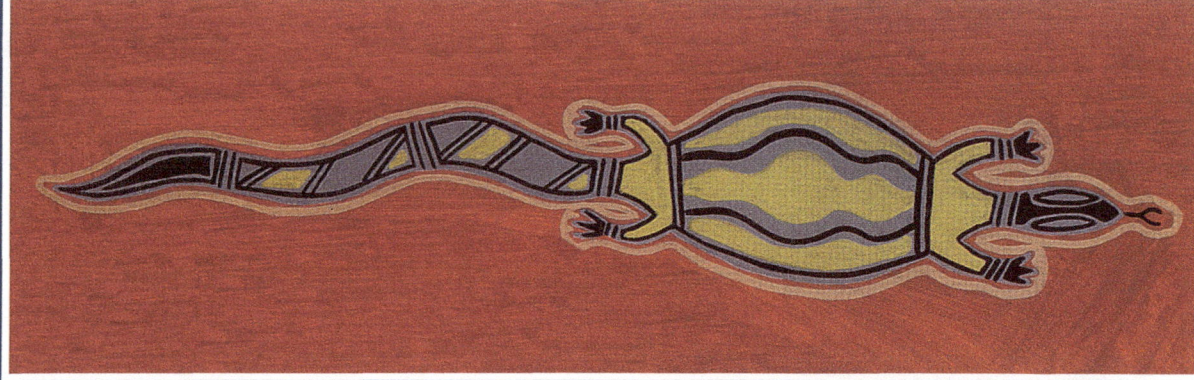

He appeared as a human being by the names of Baiame, Bunjil and Dhurramulan.

In spiritual forms as the Wandjina, Rainbow Serpent and in animal form as the Kangaroo, Emu, many other animals and within the land.

He created everything for the people and asked in return that they keep His Lores (The Covenant).

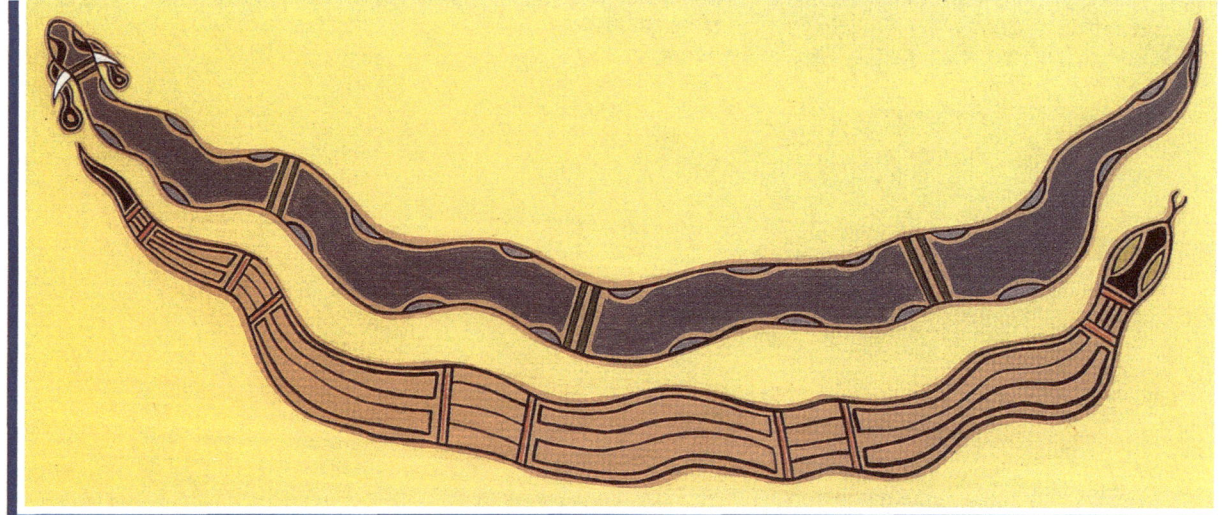

"And now regarding thy question, 'How is it that no records are to be found concerning the Prophets that have preceded Adam, the Father of Mankind, or of the kings that lived in the days of those Prophets?' Know thou that the absence of any reference to them is no proof that they did not actually exist. That no records concerning them are now available, should be attributed to their extreme remoteness, as well as to the vast changes which the earth hath undergone since their time." (Bahá'u'lláh: Gleanings, Page: 172)

With the arrival of Europeans came Christianity. They assumed that Aboriginal people did not know about God.

The Bible taught that the Serpent was evil. So, the Christians without understanding tried to destroy Aboriginal peoples belief in the Rainbow Serpent, without realising the connections.

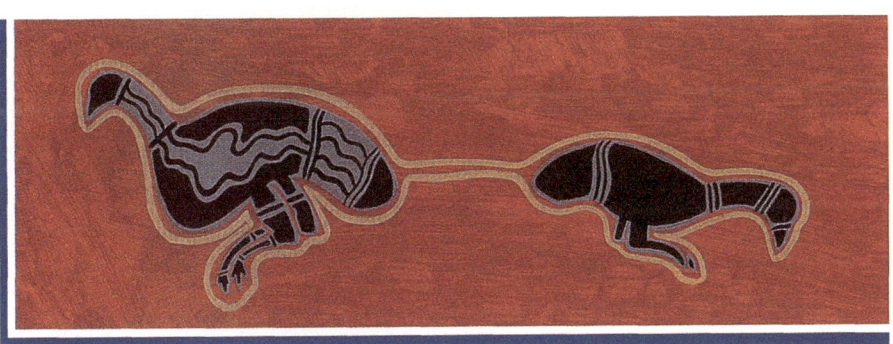

Bahá'u'lláh teaches us today that God is the All-powerful, the Great and beyond comprehension, that he doth as He pleaseth. God even spoke to Moses through the "Burning Bush".

Who are we to say that He can not appear in what ever form He pleaseth.

The Bahá'í Faith ~ An Australian Aboriginal Perspective

Adamic Cycle

Abraham, Krishna, Moses, Zoroaster, Buddha, Jesus and Muhammad

"God sends Prophets for the education of the people and the progress of mankind. Each such Manifestation of God has raised humanity. They serve the whole world by the bounty of God. The sure proof that they are the Manifestations of God is in the education and progress of the people."

('Abdu'l-Bahá: 'Abdu'l-Bahá in London, Page: 42)

In Europe and Middle-East, man's earthly desires broke the laws, which the Prophets had taught. Man's desires for power split the religions into various sects and denominations in all of the major religions.

This was due to their inability to understand the spiritual message regarding the unity of all mankind and religions. While, Aboriginal people maintained Tjukurpa - The Ancient Lore of God. With the arrival of Europeans Aboriginal people have been forced to break the lore.

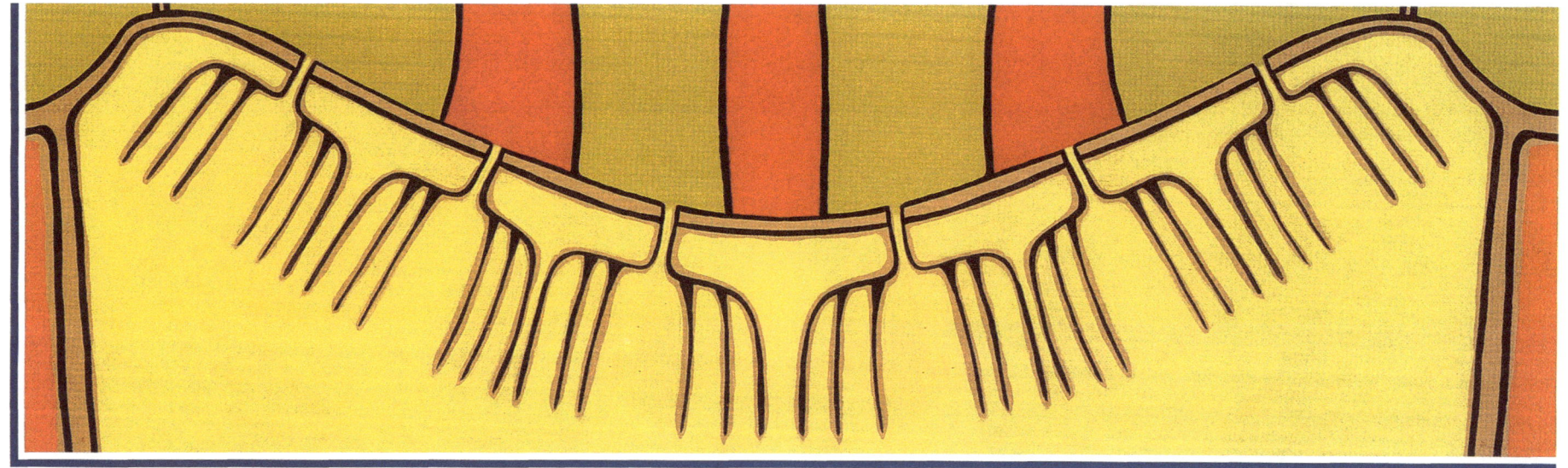

The Bahá'í Cycle

The Báb — The Gate

The Herald of the Faith

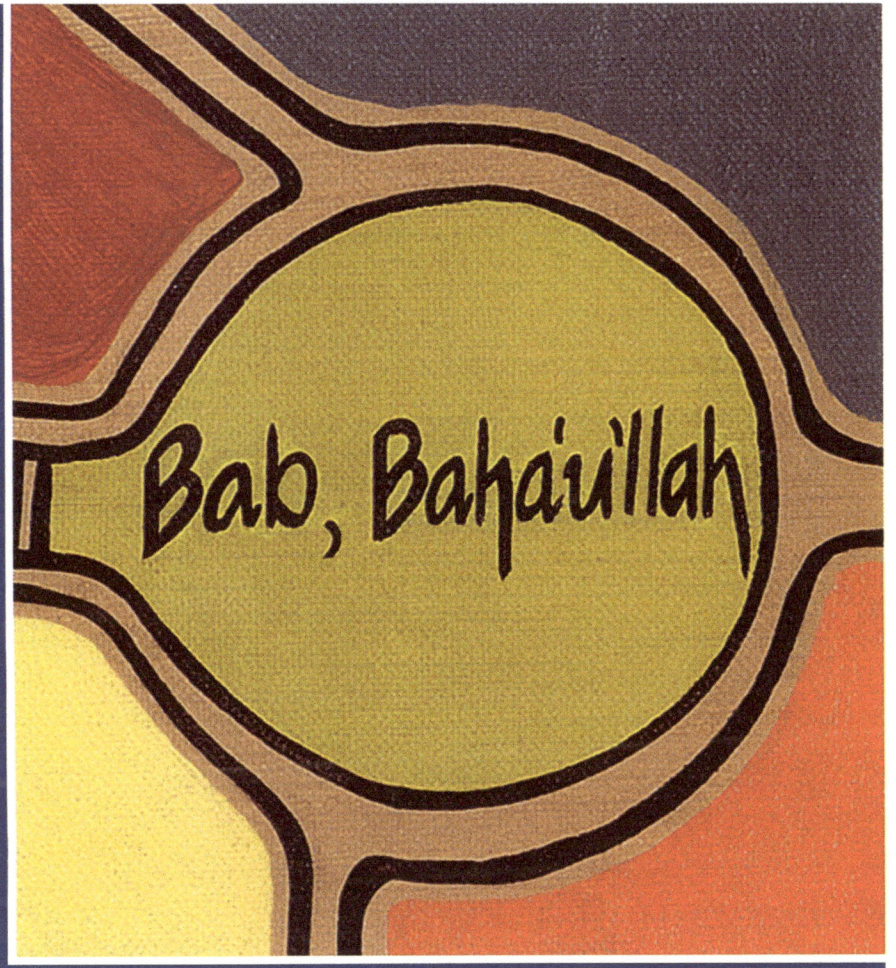

"*I am the Primal Point from which have been generated all created things. I am the Countenance of God Whose splendour can never be obscured, the Light of God Whose radiance can never fade. Whoso recognizeth Me, assurance and all good are in store for him, and whoso faileth to recognize Me, infernal fire and all evil await him*" (The Báb: Selection from the Báb, Page: 12)

To the left is the room where the Báb declared His mission

The Bahá'í Faith ~ An Australian Aboriginal Perspective

Bahá'u'lláh — The Glory of God

The Founder of the Faith

"Verily I say, this is the Day in which mankind can behold the Face, and hear the Voice, of the Promised One. The Call of God hath been raised, and the light of His countenance hath been lifted up upon men. It behoveth every man to blot out the trace of every idle word from the tablet of his heart, and to gaze, with an open and unbiased mind, on the signs of His Revelation, the proofs of His Mission, and the tokens of His glory. Great indeed is this Day!" *(Bahá'u'lláh: Gleanings, Pages: 10-11)*

The Divine Lote-Tree

"O thou who hast turned away from God! Wert thou to look with the eye of fairness upon the Divine Lote-Tree, thou wouldst perceive the marks of thy sword on its boughs, and its branches, and its leaves, notwithstanding that God created thee for the purpose of recognizing and of serving it." *(Bahá'u'lláh: Epistle to the Son of the Wolf, Page: 84)*

Some Principles from the Teachings of Bahá'u'lláh

- The Independent Investigation of Truth,
- The Unity of Mankind,
- The Unity of Religion and Science,
- Abolition of all forms of Prejudices,
- Equality of Women and Men,
- Universal Peace,
- Non-Interference of Religion and Politics,
- Equality of Sexes,
- Universal Education.

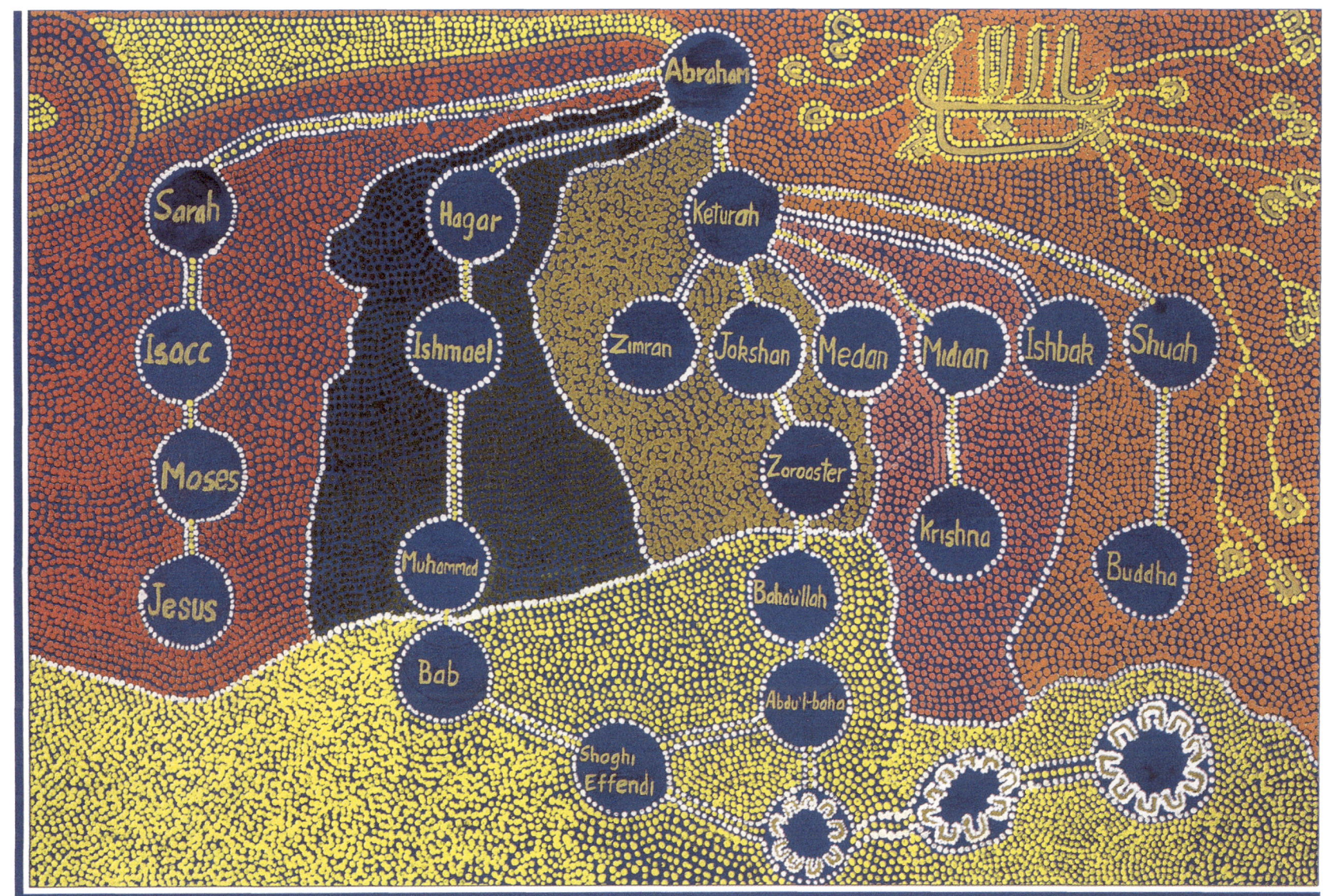

The painting on the left depicts the lineage of some of the Founders of world religions

Far left shows the gardens surrounding the resting place of Bahá'u'lláh

The Bahá'í Faith ~ An Australian Aboriginal Perspective

'Abdu'l-Bahá

The Master

"Bahá'u'lláh, in the Book of His Covenant, appointed 'Abdu'l-Bahá, His eldest son, as the Centre of His Covenant and the Head of the Faith."

(Bahá'u'lláh: Kitáb-i-Aqdas: Notes, Page: 196)

'Abdu'l-Bahá was responsible for interpreting the Writings of Bahá'u'lláh.

"Bahá'u'lláh has Himself revealed its principles, established its institutions, appointed the person to interpret His Word and conferred the necessary authority on the body designed to supplement and apply His legislative ordinances."

(Shoghi Effendi: World Order of Bahá'u'lláh, Page: 145)

'Abdu'l-Bahá addressed Members of the White Race

"...I hope that ye may cause that downtrodden race to become glorious, and to be joined with the white race, to serve the world of man with the utmost sincerity, faithfulness, love, and purity. This opposition, enmity, and prejudice among the white race and the coloured cannot be effaced except through faith, assurance, and the teachings of the Blessed Beauty... This question of the union of the white and the black is very important, for if it is not realized, erelong great difficulties will arise, and harmful results will follow ... enmity will be increased day by day, and the final result will be hardship and may end in bloodshed." *('Abdu'l-Bahá: quoted in The Advent of Divine Justice, p. 39)*

The House of 'Abdu'l-Bahá in the Holy Land

Shoghi Effendi

The Guardian

" 'Abdu'l-Bahá, in His Will and Testament, appointed Shoghi Effendi, His eldest grandson, as the Guardian and Head of the Faith."

(Bahá'u'lláh: Kitáb-i-Aqdas: Notes, Pages: 196-197)

Shoghi Effendi was responsible for the establishment of the Administrative Order of the Bahá'í Faith.

Based on the writings of Bahá'u'lláh, Shoghi Effendi used 'The Eagle' in Bahá'í gardens as a totem.

"I am reminded, on this historic occasion, of the significant words uttered by Bahá'u'lláh Himself, Who as attested by the Center of the Covenant, in His Writings, "compared the colored people to the black pupil of the eye," through which "the light of the spirit shineth forth."

"I feel particularly gratified by the substantial participation in this epoch-making conference of the members of a race dwelling in a continent which for the most part has retained its primitive simplicity and remained uncontaminated by the evils of a gross, a rampant and cancerous materialism undermining the fabric of human society alike in the East and in the West."

(Shoghi Effendi: Messages to the Bahá'í World, Page: 136)

The Guardian's resting place

The Bahá'í Faith ~ An Australian Aboriginal Perspective

Unity of all Religions

The Prophets and their Religions

Aboriginal Lore	Each tribe had its own Lore, but the underlying principles are the same
Abraham	Unknown
Krishna	Hinduism
Moses	Judaism
Zoroaster	Zoroastrianism
Buddha	Buddhism
Jesus	Christianity
Muhammad	Islam
The Báb	The Bábí Faith
Bahá'u'lláh	Bahá'í Faith

"Be as one spirit, one soul, leaves of one tree, flowers of one garden, waves of one ocean."

"The holy Manifestations Who have been the Sources or Founders of the various religious systems were united and agreed in purpose and teaching. Abraham, Moses, Zoroaster, Buddha, Jesus, Muhammad, the Báb and Bahá'u'lláh are one in spirit and reality. Moreover, each Prophet fulfilled the promise of the One Who came before Him and, likewise, Each announced the One Who would follow.

Consider how Abraham foretold the coming of Moses, and Moses embodied the Abrahamic statement. Moses prophesied the Messianic cycle, and Christ fulfilled the law of Moses.

It is evident, therefore, that the Holy Manifestations Who founded the religious systems are united and agreed; there is no differentiation possible in Their mission and teachings; all are reflectors of reality, and all are promulgators of the religion of God.

The divine religion is reality, and reality is not multiple; it is one. Therefore, the foundations of the religious systems are one because all proceed from the indivisible reality; but the followers of these systems have disagreed; discord, strife and warfare have arisen among them, for they have forsaken the foundation and held to that which is but imitation and semblance."

`Abdu'l-Bahá: Promulgation of Universal Peace, Pages: 197-198

The Bahá'í Faith ~ An Australian Aboriginal Perspective

"Beware, O believers in the Unity of God, lest ye be tempted to make any distinction between any of the Manifestations of His Cause, or to discriminate against the signs that have accompanied and proclaimed their Revelation"

Unity of Mankind and Colonisation

"The Great Being saith: O ye children of men! The fundamental purpose animating the Faith of God and His Religion is to safeguard the interests and promote the unity of the human race, and to foster the spirit of love and fellowship amongst men. Suffer it not to become a source of dissension and discord, of hate and enmity. This is the straight Path, the fixed and immovable foundation. Whatsoever is raised on this foundation, the changes and chances of the world can never impair its strength, nor will the revolution of countless centuries undermine its structure."

Bahá'u'lláh: Gleanings, Page: 215

To understand "The fundamental purpose animating the Faith of God" and Colonisation, which is the unity of mankind, puts a different perspective on the colonisation of our country.

Although, we may not agree with the way in which our country was colonised. It did not have to happen in the way that it did, had the Christians followed the true teachings of Christ, which was to "Love thy Neighbour".

The colonial history of Australia has been a very difficult period for Aboriginal people, who are still faced with all forms of oppression, racism, dispossession of our land, separation from families and loss of human rights etc. Bahá'u'lláh teaches us today to rise above these crises and to embrace this new Spiritual Lore for today.

"The well-being of mankind, its peace and security, are unattainable unless and until its unity is firmly established."

Bahá'u'lláh: Kitáb-i-Aqdas: Other Sections, Page: 11

The Bahá'í Faith ~ An Australian Aboriginal Perspective

The Bahá'í Faith ~ An Australian Aboriginal Perspective

The Bahá'í World Centre

"And it shall come to pass in the last days, that the mountain of the Lord's house shall be established in the top of the mountain, and shall be exalted above the hills; and all nations shall flow unto it."

Isaiah; Coming of Christ's Kingdom Prophesised; Chapter 2: The Holy Bible, King James

"Call out to Zion, O Carmel, and announce the joyful tidings: He that was hidden from mortal eyes is come! Ere long will God sail His Ark upon thee, and will manifest the people of Bahá."

(Bahá'u'lláh: Tablets of Bahá'u'lláh, Page: 5)

This painting represents the Terraces of the Shrine of the Báb, the Shrine of Bahá'u'lláh and the Universal House of Justice, with the Rainbow Serpent coming out of the Shrine of Bahá'u'lláh with a renewed Spiritual Lore, taking the message to Aboriginal people, animals and the land.

Totems of Aboriginal People

Aboriginal people have a number of totems, which have a spiritual link to certain animals and places in the land.

From an Aboriginal perspective, all animals brought the Spiritual Lores to assist man to survive and understand the meaning of these Lores.

This process is now called the "Progressive Revelation", each bringing a different Lore, stories of our creation.

From this perspective, some of the Prophets had totems; Jesus (The Fish), Noah (The Dove with an olive branch).

Bahá'u'lláh's Totem: He said;

"**I am the royal Falcon on the arm of the Almighty.**"

The Shrine of Bahá'u'lláh

A part of the painting representing the Shrine of Bahá'u'lláh and a photograph of the Shrine of Bahá'u'lláh.

The Bahá'í Faith ~ An Australian Aboriginal Perspective

The Shrine of the Báb

"And many people shall go and say, Come ye, and let us go up to the mountain of the Lord, to the house of the God of Jacob; and he will teach us of his ways, and we will walk in his paths: for out Zion shall go forth the law, and the word of the Lord from Jerusalem."

Isaiah; Coming of Christ's Kingdom Prophesied; Chapter 2: The Holy Bible, King James

The Bahá'í Faith ~ An Australian Aboriginal Perspective

The Terraces of the Shrine of the Báb

"Twin luminaries that heralded the advent of the Faith of the Báb", prophesied that at the appearance of the Promised One all things would be reversed, the last would be first, the first last."

Bahá'u'lláh: Kitáb-i-Aqdas: Notes, Pages: 239-240

A painting representing the Terraces of the Shrine of the Báb and a photo of the Terraces of the Shrine of the Báb. In our eyes the Terraces of the Shrine of the Báb also presents a connection to Tjukurpa - the Ancient Cycle and the Bahá'í Cycle.

The Royal Falcon

Preparation for Entry by Troops

"I am the Royal Falcon on the arm of the Almighty."

—Bahá'u'lláh

This painting represents when people learn more about the Bahá'í Faith and its teachings and they decide to join, which is the process of Entry by Troops.

"The advent of the day which, as prophesied by Abdu'l-Bahá, will witness the entry by troops of peoples of divers nations and races into the Bahá'í world - a day which, viewed in its proper perspective, will be the prelude to that long-awaited hour when a mass conversion on the part of these same nations and races, ... will suddenly revolutionise the fortunes of the Faith."

Shoghi Effendi: Citadel of Faith, Page: 117

The Bahá'í Faith ~ An Australian Aboriginal Perspective

Ancient System – New Administrative Order – Community Lifestyle

This painting represents the connection between the Ancient System, which is/was strictly administered and adhered to by the Elders and members of the community for thousands of years. The Community lifestyle of Aboriginal people as we see it is embodied within the Bahá'í community lifestyle, while the Bahá'í Administrative Order is a completely new administrative system.

Ancient Kinship System - Skin Names

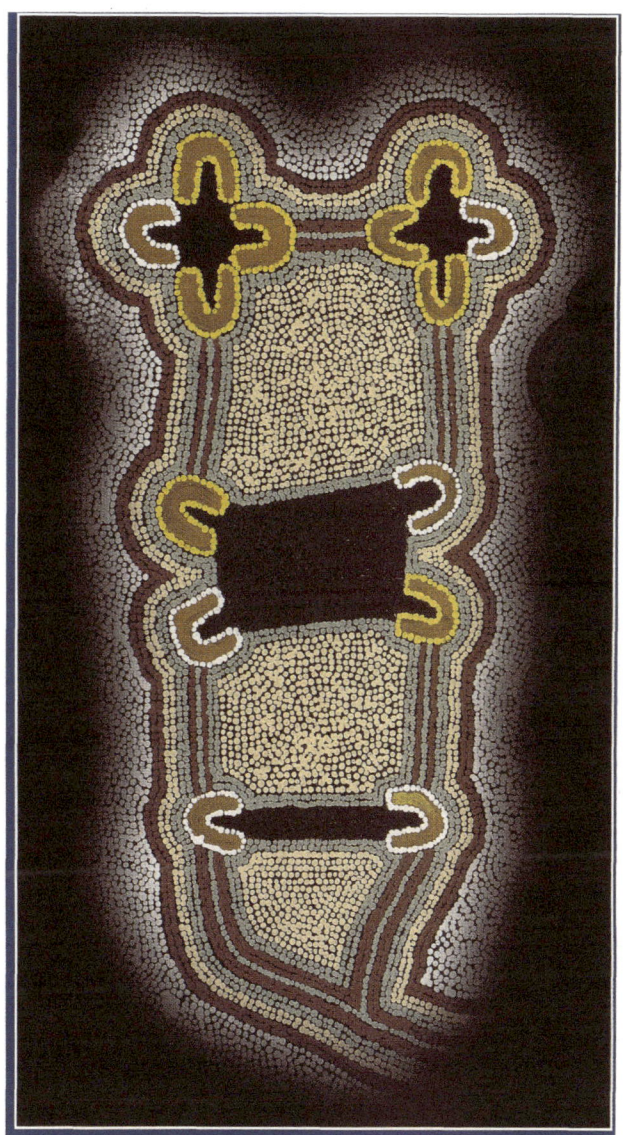

"'Abdu'l-Bahá has written that the more distant the blood-relationship between the couple the better, since such marriages provide the basis for the physical well-being of humanity and are conducive to fellowship among mankind."

(Universal House of Justice Aqdas: Notes, Pages: 222-223)

The Kinship System (Skin Names) which Aboriginal people have kept intact for thousands of years is like the blood-relation system that Abdul-Bahá teaches us in the statement above.

There are three distinct systems that overlap each other: the Eight Section System, Four Section System and the Two Sides.

By marrying according to their blood-relationship, this ensures that their relationships are not compromised in the event of trouble arising between various families groups and tribes from one end of the country to the other.

This also ensures the survival of each particular blood-line and language group. Each System has two sides to ensure that the spiritual balance is maintained within the community.

The Two Sides of the Kinship Systems – Skin Names

The term used by anthropologist to classify the two sides as Moieties.

Moiety Group A – Skin Names	Moiety Group B – Skin Names
8 Subsection System	**8 Subsection System**
Tjungala – Nungala	Tjampitjin – Nampitjin
Tjungoray – Nungoray	Tjapangarti – Napangarti
Tjapanangka – Napanangka	Tjakamarra – Nakamarra
Tjupurala – Napurula	Tjapiljarri – Napiljarri
4 Subsection System	**4 Subsection System**
Banbari	Wungu
Kurugeila	Guburu
Two Sides Subsection System	**Two Sides Subsection System**
Jungaru	Widtaru

Ancient Kinship System - 8 Subsections (Skin Names)

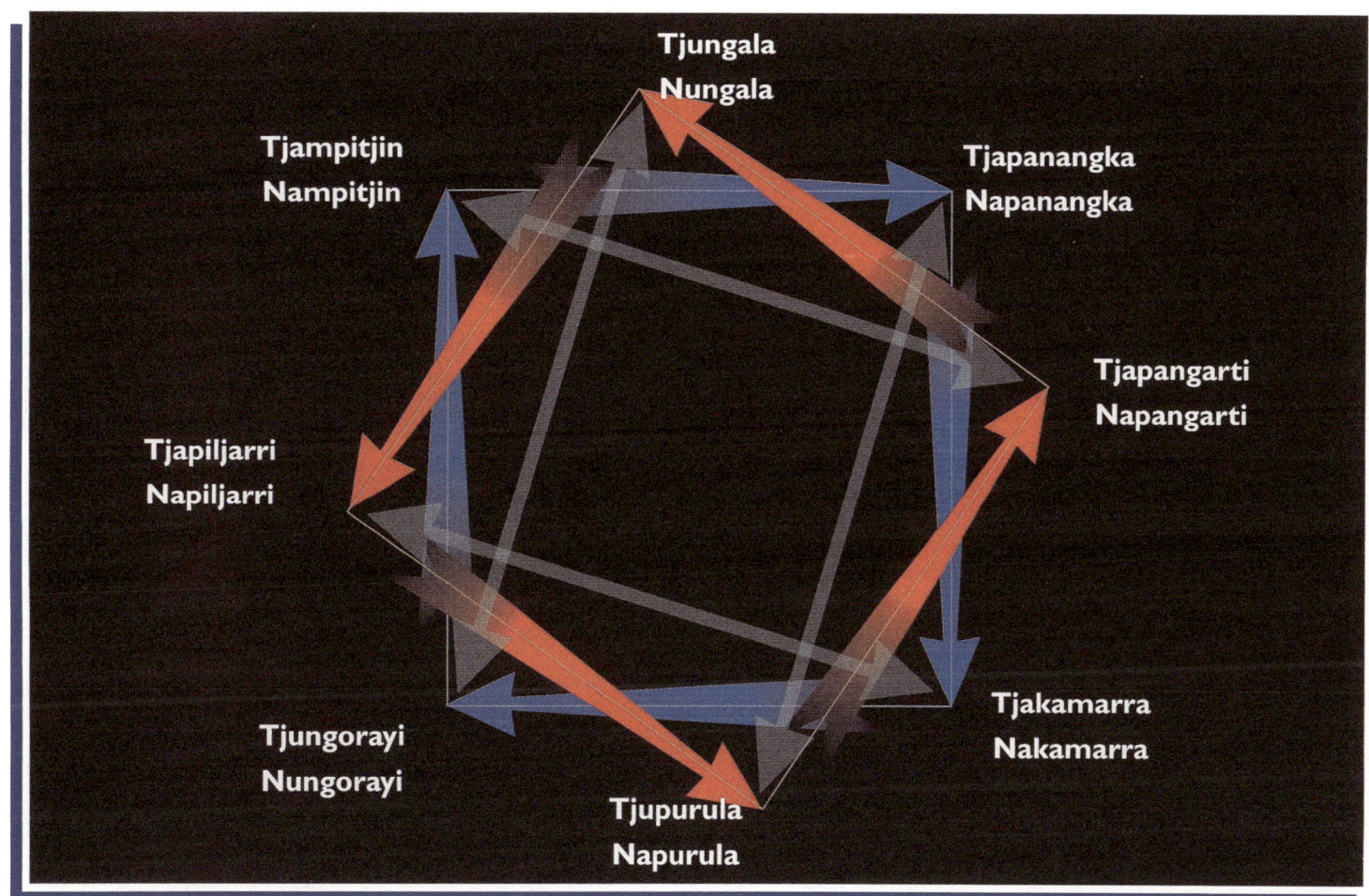

In each of the Kinship Systems, the Skin name is given to you by your mother.

The blue and red lines indicated the direction from mother to children, which goes four generations and starts again.

The transparent lines are the straight marriage lines.

The Bahá'í Faith ~ An Australian Aboriginal Perspective

Ancient Kinship System - 4 Subsection (Skin Names)

In each Kinship System, the parents are on the opposite side of their children. Each group is responsible for their particular side, which is with their respective grandparents, brothers and brother-in-law. The same process also happens with Women's Lore.

Ancient System - Two Sides

Elders are on both sides of the systems to ensure that the correct guidance and procedures are followed.

Although, this particular System does not have any Skin Names, people just use the names of the Two Sides.

The 8 Subsection and 4 Subsection Systems also have names for their two sides.

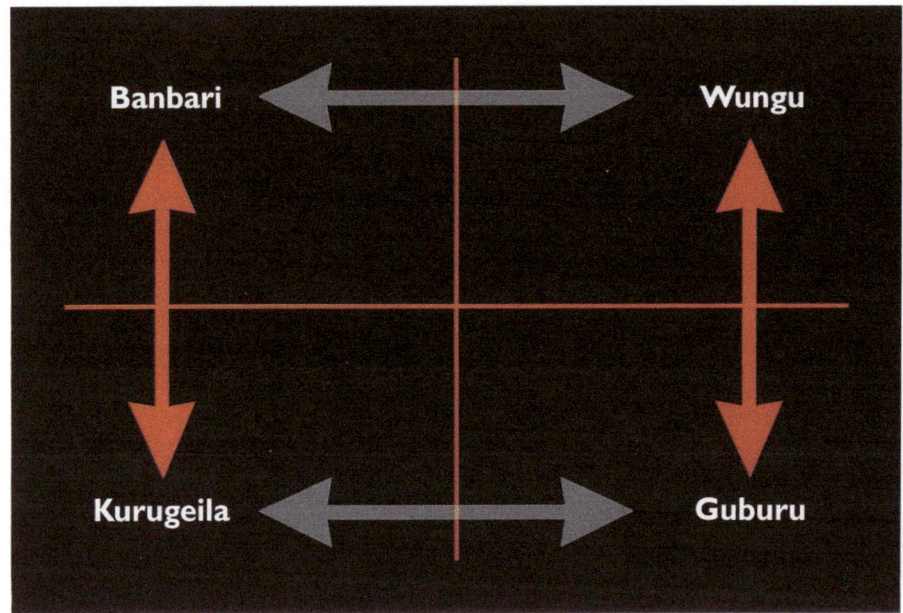

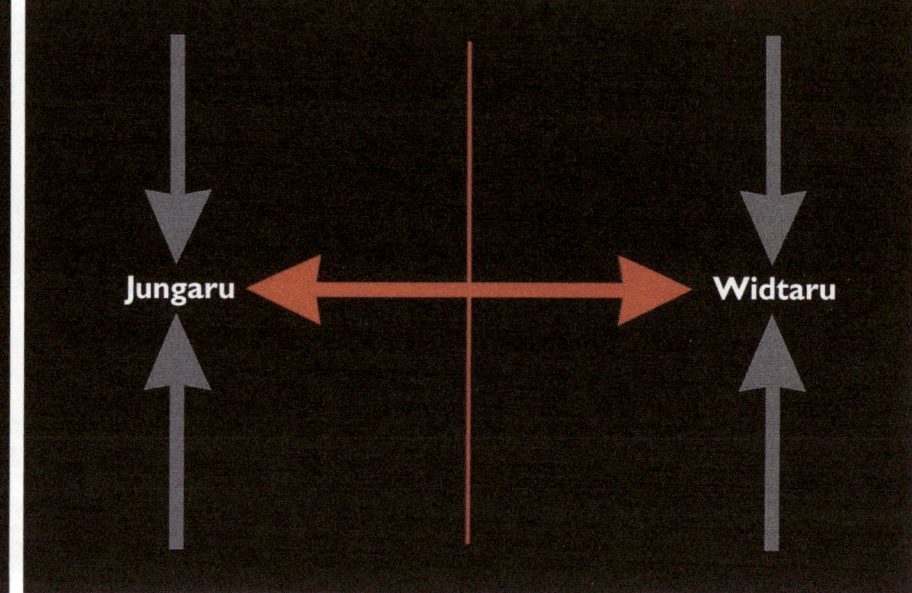

Community Lifestyle

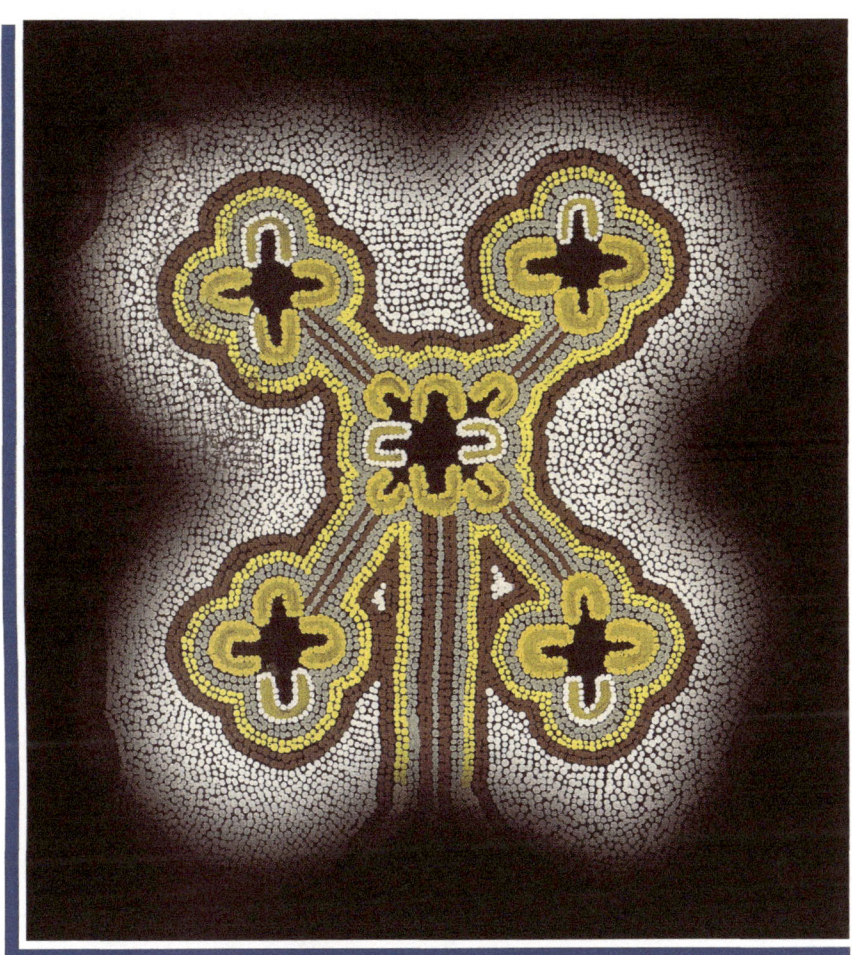

The Kinship System incorporates an individual's place in society. It instills a sense of belonging and no-one is left out.

The skin name also determines your relationship to the community, where you sit and who you can marry etc., it promotes, strengthens and unifies the community through the kinship system.

It promotes mutual care and respect for one another, which is the basis of all community people/ families lifestyle.

If certain problems arise in a family group, it is the responsibility of the family to deal with the issues before it affects the community.

The Elders/Counsellors/ ABM (represented in white) play a major role in establishing order and giving guidance to the community.

This System has the capabilities of correcting certain proper/improper behaviour between individuals, families groups and tribes.

Individuals have certain rights, responsibilities and obligations to the family, community, protection of land, teaching the songs, stories, language and dances, which is passed onto the next generation.

Great importance, awareness and respect is given to keeping our cultural heritage.

The Bahá'í Faith ~ An Australian Aboriginal Perspective

The Spiritual Principles of Aboriginal Lore and Society

Aboriginal people have survived in the entire different climatic environment from the Deserts, Rain Forests, Tropical Islands, Snowy Mountains, Woodlands, Wetlands, Plains and Savannahs.

The ability to adapt to the environment has meant the maintenance and survival of its people, languages, social systems, lore and cultures. The basis for our survival has been the "Spiritual Principles", which is a simple belief in the Creator, who gave us our Social, Spiritual Lores and the responsibilities of custodianship - meaning living in harmony with each other and nature (animals, plants and land).

As custodians, each family, language group or tribe is responsible for their particular part of their stories or connections to the various scared sites, stories, lores, ceremonies, culture and land that connects one tribe to another (like a jigsaw puzzle) and extends throughout the whole country.

To ensure the maintenance of a strict code of behavior in the community the members had to know what effect an individual's action would have upon the whole social and spiritual well-being of the community and environment. Depending upon the seriousness of the issues caused by an individual meant that it had to be dealt with in both a social and spiritual way to keep balance within the community.

Although there are many families groups (kinship system), languages and tribes, the one uniting force with all Aboriginal people is the spiritual connection to each other.

Tjukurpa

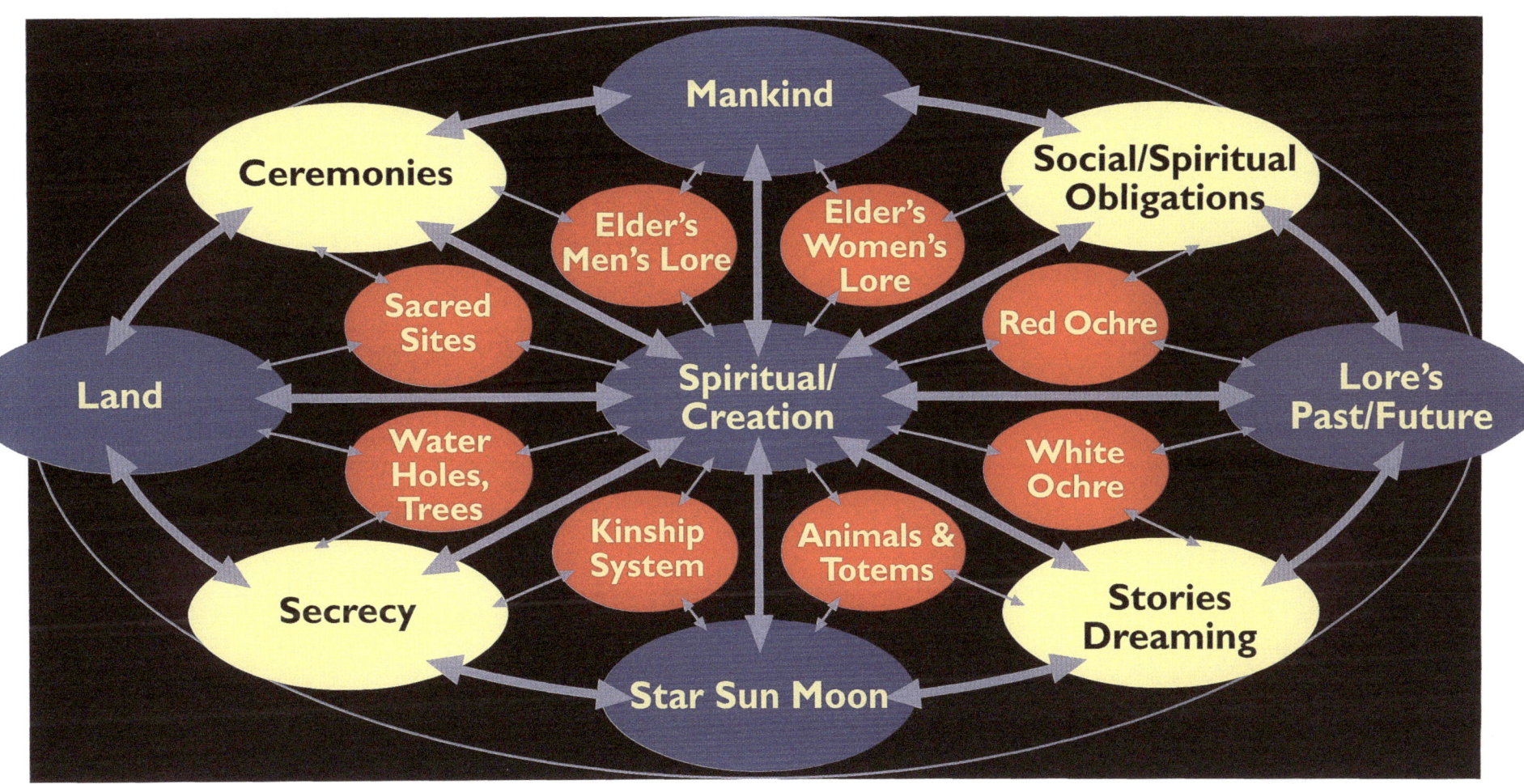

The Bahá'í Faith ~ An Australian Aboriginal Perspective

New Administrative Order

"The world's equilibrium hath been upset through the vibrating influence of this most great, this new World Order. Mankind's ordered life hath been revolutionized through the agency of this unique, this wondrous System - the like of which mortal eyes have never witnessed."

Bahá'u'lláh: The Kitab-i-Aqdas, Page: 85

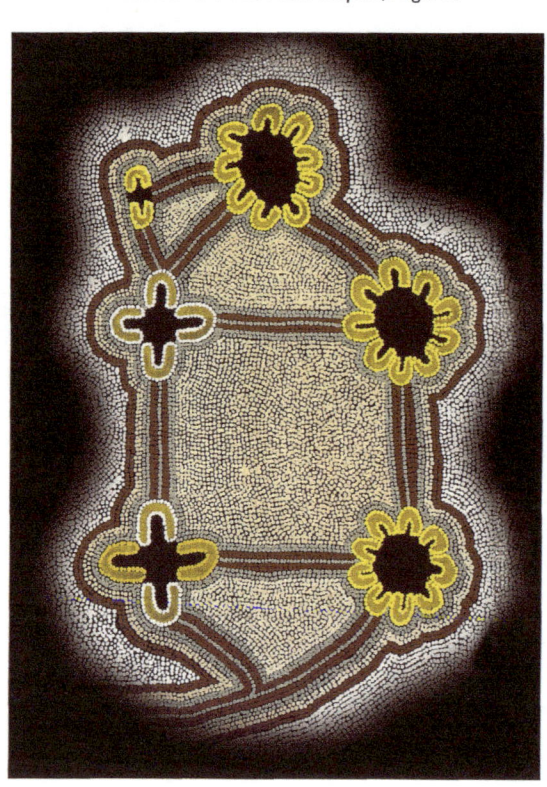

Institution of the Counsellors Arm of the Learned

The Universal House of Justice appoints the Counsellor members of the International Teaching Centre and the Continental Counsellors. Members of Auxiliary Boards are appointed by the Continental Counsellors. All these individuals fall within the definition of the "learned" given by Shoghi Effendi.

Bahá'u'lláh: Kitáb-i-Aqdas: Notes, Page: 246

Elected Arm

'Abdu'l-Bahá, in His Will and Testament, outlines the method to be pursued for the election of the House of Justice.
An institution which is to be elected in a locality whenever there are nine or more resident adult Bahá'ís.
Local and Secondary Houses of Justice are, for the present, known as Local Spiritual Assemblies and National Spiritual Assemblies.

Bahá'u'lláh: Kitáb-i-Aqdas: Notes, Pages: 188-189

The Bahá'í Faith ~ An Australian Aboriginal Perspective

Election Process of the Bahá'í Faith

There is No electioneering! No nominations! No discussion on who to vote for! No how to vote pamphlets! And No party politics!

It is easy to understand the process of election for the members of the Local Spiritual Assembly, the National Spiritual Assembly and the Universal House of Justice in terms of Aboriginal Social and Spiritual Lores. The Election Process of the Bahá'í Faith is, basically, a simple process in reverence, prayer and devotions to the will of God.

O ye Men of Justice!

It has been elucidated in the writings of 'Abdu'l-Bahá and Shoghi Effendi that, while the membership of the Universal House of Justice is confined to men, both women and men are eligible for election to Secondary and Local Houses of Justice*.

Bahá'u'lláh: Kitáb-i-Aqdas: Notes, Page 201

* Currently designated as National and Local Spiritual Assemblies.

No one asks to be elected onto the Assemblies or be given these responsibilities.

The process of election/selection is the same process as in Aboriginal communities, when Assembly Members/Elders are chosen by the community, which is one who has the right spiritual qualities, who can deal with all social and spiritual matters that arise in the community.

The Assembly Members/Elders are given the responsibility to perform certain tasks; teach certain lores, ceremonies, songs, stories, cater for sections of land and to protect the interests of the whole community on all matters, whether they are Bahá'ís or not.

The Bahá'í Faith ~ An Australian Aboriginal Perspective

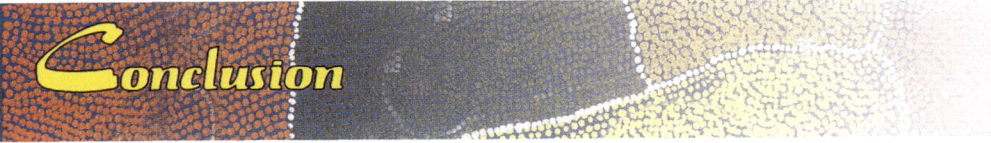

Conclusion

It is hoped that this booklet has given you a better understanding and insight of the Bahá'í Faith from an Australian Aboriginal and Torres Strait Islander Perspective.

"... RECALL WITH PROFOUND EMOTION MESSAGE BELOVED GUARDIAN OCCASION 1953 CONFERENCE WHEREIN HE EXTOLLED PUREHEARTED SPIRITUALLY RECEPTIVE INDIGENOUS PEOPLE AFRICA WHOM BAHÁ'U'LLÁH COMPARED PUPIL EYE THROUGH WHICH LIGHT OF SPIRIT SHINETH FORTH AND FOR WHOSE CONVERSION BOTH GUARDIAN AND MASTER BEFORE HIM YEARNED AND LABOURED ..."

From a cable of the Universal House of Justice

Acknowledgements

It is with great appreciation that I wish to acknowledge many of the people, my Lore Brothers and communities namely: Woorabinda, Palm Island, Billiluna, Mulan, Balgo and Fitzroy Crossing. All of whom have been a part of and have greatly assisted in teaching me Traditional Aboriginal Lore.

Colin Daisy (Tjakamarra)
Boxer Milner (Tjampitjin)
Blucher Tjapiljarri
Speiler Sturt (Tjampitjin)
Fitler Smith (Tjapiljarri)
Robert Bundle (Guburu)
Billy Joe Munns (Banbari)
Anthony Freeman (Kurugeila)
Beau Freeman (Kurugeila)
Kumanjay (Raymond) Chungala (Tjampitjin)
Kumanjay (Fred Johnson - Guburu)
Linda Charmawina (Napangarti)
Chamia Samual (Napurula)
Napangarti
Palmer Gordon (Tjpaanangka)

Jack Gordon (Tjampitjin)
Minne Pye (Nakamarra)
Marie Gordon (Nakamarra)
Robert Mackay (Tjungoray)
George Wallaby (Tjungala)
Michael Charmawina (Tjungala)
Ivan Tjapangarti
Jimmy Chooga (Tjanpangarti)
Joshua Kungah (Tjakamarra)
Eddie Tjampitjin
Rex Tjampitjin
Boxer Billliluna (Tjapanangka)
Lulu Napangarti
Patsy Mudgedel (Nakamarra)
Philip Nungoray (Tjampitjin)

PAINTINGS

Cover Painting by Colin Daisy
Progressive Revelation design by Philip Obah - painted by Patrick Williams
Entry by Troops by Colin Daisy
Divine Lote Tree, World Centre, Ancient System, Community Lifestyle and Bahá'í Administration by Philip Obah
Brochure designed by Faizi designs - Brisbane

Philip Obah © 2002

www.ingramcontent.com/pod-product-compliance
Lightning Source LLC
Chambersburg PA
CBHW041950150426

43193CB00004B/54